T0099915

The Totality of Now

30 techniques to achieve inner peace and live in the now

Dr Melanie O'Shea

BALBOA
PRESS
A DIVISION OF HAY HOUSE

Website: drmelanieoshea.com

Balboa Press books may be ordered through booksellers or by contacting:

Balboa Press
A Division of Hay House
1663 Liberty Drive
Bloomington, IN 47403
www.balboapress.com.au
1 (877) 407-4847

The information, ideas, and suggestions in this book are not intended
as a substitute for professional advice. Before following any suggestions
contained in this book, you should consult your personal physician or mental
health professional. Neither the author nor the publisher shall be liable or
responsible for any loss or damage allegedly arising as a consequence of
your use or application of any information or suggestions in this book.

Print information available on the last page.

ISBN: 978-1-4525-0879-5 (sc)
ISBN: 978-1-4525-0880-1 (e)

Balboa Press rev. date: 03/13/2013

CONTENTS

ARTWORK

Book cover From Core Energy Series 2012:
Sesuvium portulacastrum . . . antifungal . . .

A rtist, Renata Buziak, engages nature and organic processes in her experimental photographic image making process: the biochrome. Renata received a number of art awards and presented her work nationally and internationally in solo and group exhibitions. In 2006, she was the Artist-in-Residence at the Brisbane Botanic Gardens Mt Coot-tha, and in 2012 at the Caloundra Art Gallery. Renata's work is held in public and private collections including Mater Hospital, Sunsuper, Griffith University, ASP Warsaw, Redlands Gallery, South Bank Corporation, and The Daryl Hewson Collection. In April 2010, the Queensland Centre for Photography (QCP) launched Renata Buziak's 'Afterimage' publication, with a foreword by Lyle Rexer and essay by Dr Victoria Garnons-Williams.

In 2006, Renata completed her Bachelor of Photography with First Class Honours at Queensland College of Art (QCA) Griffith University, Brisbane, where she is currently undertaking her PhD studies. She is a sessional staff member at Griffith and a board member at the Queensland Centre for Photography.

Website: renata-buziak.com

ACKNOWLEDGEMENTS

Thank you to all my wonderful clients, family, and friends. You are all my greatest teachers. Each and every day, you teach me about myself, and about life. I believe that we go on learning until the day our bodies die. It is so wonderful to connect with other spirits on our journey through life. I enjoy the interactions with each and every person who I attract into my work life, and personal life. We are all on a magical and often challenging journey, where we can choose to evolve as human beings and spiritual beings. I continue to enjoy learning and growing, and I hope that everyone I come in contact with is committed to seeing the magic in their life journey too. You, the reader, are also on this journey with me. Thank you for joining me on this journey of learning and discovery.

INTRODUCTION

I often ask my clients—what if you only have 5, 10, 20 years to live? This is a thought provoking and confronting question. We often forget that life is short, and can end at any time. Often 5, 10, 20 years is a realistic estimate for some individuals. This reality check is a blessing in disguise as we are reminded that we need to resolve any issues that are holding us back. We can truly embrace and enjoy life, and learn how to get joy out of the simple things in life. We can learn to live in **the totality of now**. We can practice mindfulness, which is the act of being in the now. We often lose sight of the fact that we are blessed with five wonderful senses—sight, hearing, smell, taste, and touch. As opposed to just taking these senses for granted, we need to see the beautiful sights before our eyes, hear nature around us, smell the roses, taste food and drink mindfully, and enjoy the comfort associated with having a sense of touch. Let's get back to basics, and be in the moment. It is perfectly fine to look forward to the future, and have hopes and dreams, but we also need to learn to be in the present day. Life is not only about focusing on the past or the future. We can allow ourselves to enjoy our lives right now too. I hope you are able to consider the strategies I have suggested in order to live a more satisfying life, and gain the inner peace you truly deserve. Unlike any other guide to mental wellbeing, this guide is unique as it has 30 simple, easy to follow, achievable strategies to achieve a sense of wellbeing.

Have a great day,

Dr Melanie O'Shea

HOW TO USE THIS BOOK

Prior to starting this book, I would recommend that you buy yourself a good quality hard cover exercise book, and some good quality pens. Once you have made these purchases, you will be prepared to start the exercises. The beauty of keeping a hard cover exercise book is that you can keep all the exercises you have completed in the one place. You can use your exercise book as a personal development resource, which you add to from time to time. Furthermore, this book can be treasured in times to come, as you will be able to reflect on your growth during your human and spiritual journey.

Once you are prepared with your writing tools, you can begin the journey. Perhaps you might like to read this book first, looking at each and every exercise. Following this, pick an exercise on a regular basis, say once per week, and make a commitment to working through an exercise each week. You do not need to commit to any particular order in terms of completing the exercises. In fact, you are the master of your own destiny as to what order you would like to complete the exercises.

Enjoy the journey of completing the exercise. Treat the completion of each exercise as a fun, and insightful experience. I wish you all the best for your journey into learning to appreciate the totality of now. May you achieve the inner peace you have been longing for, and enjoy living life in the now.

I can learn to think in a more rational way. This helps me make less impulsive choices.

E ach day we appear to have hundreds of thoughts. However, for the most part, we are largely unaware of these thoughts. That's because thoughts are often fleeting in that they come and go so quickly. These fleeting thoughts are often referred to as 'automatic thoughts'. Thoughts have a dramatic impact on how we feel about our family, friends, partner, acquaintances, strangers, the world, and ourselves. These internal thoughts affect our behaviour, and experience of the world. This concept of thoughts having a direct impact on our emotions and behaviour is well known in spiritual, psychological, and metaphysical teachings.

In psychological terms, adaptive thoughts are often referred to as 'rational thoughts', and maladaptive thoughts are often referred to as 'irrational thoughts'. Challenging irrational thoughts is commonly referred to as 'Cognitive Restructuring', which is a core component of the evidence-based psychological therapy known as Cognitive Behavioural Therapy (CBT). A simplistic approach to changing irrational thoughts into rational thoughts is to simply record these irrational thoughts, and then come up with rational alternatives. See example.

Negative Thought	Positive Thought Challenge
Write down your negative thought	➤ **Come up with a more realistic thought. Some questions that might help you with this process include-** ➤ **What's the evidence for this thought? Is there a more helpful thought?** ➤ **If a friend or a loved one had this thought, what advice would I give?**
I'm a total failure	➤ There is no evidence that I'm a total failure. Sure, I've made some mistakes in my life, or learnt some lessons, but who hasn't?
I made a mistake again	➤ Sometimes making mistakes is the only way in which we learn. Learning is a part of life.
I will never get anywhere in life	➤ I'm learning that life does not always go to plan, but I am taking it one day at a time.
I can't cope with life anymore	➤ Sometimes I feel overwhelmed by life, but I usually feel better after a while.

NOTES

I am grateful for each and every day. Each day we can identify some positive things that happen in our lives.

KEEP A DAILY GRATITUDE LIST

2

Sometimes it's just too easy to wake up in the morning and think that it's just another day, and a potentially mundane day at that! This form of negative thinking can lead us to miss out on the magic in life. It exists, but often we have to look closely. Life can be hectic, and sometimes we can lose sight of the fact that we have people in our lives who love and care about us. Have you ever looked at your loved ones and wondered what life would be like if they were not around anymore? For most of us, this is a undesirable thought, and not the sort of negative thinking we wish to entertain. However, my point is that it's important to appreciate the loved ones on our life journey. With the hustle, bustle, and stress of life, we often fail to appreciate the ones closest to our hearts. Not only do we neglect to appreciate and acknowledge our loved ones, sometimes we stop noticing the wonderful and magical things that happen to us each and every day. Keeping a daily gratitude list helps keep our positive life experiences in perspective. A daily gratitude list takes only a few minutes at the end of each day, and perhaps you might choose to keep a hardbound diary, as opposed to a list. This can be a wonderful keepsake in months, or even years to come. Examples of experiences you might record in the daily gratitude list include cooking a special meal, a smile from a stranger, enjoying a fresh fruit juice, a walk in the sun, and a hug from a loved one.

I speak to myself positively.
I no longer beat myself
up, and I feel happier.

USE POSITIVE SELF-TALK

3

Positive self-talk can be described as positive self-statements about ourselves, or statements about what we want (wish for) in our lives. These statements can be said out loud (if appropriate!), or perhaps more appropriately to ourselves. You can pick a statement about yourself based on an issue you would like to work on. For example, perhaps you are single and have not been successful in romantic relationships recently. Perhaps this situation might have resulted, in part, through negative self-dialogue. An example of this might be "I'll be single forever!", "I'm unlovable". To counteract this maladaptive negative thinking, you might choose a statement such as, "I am loving and loveable". Perhaps you simply want to make an affirmation about what you would like in your life, such as more money, for example. You might have an affirmation such as "Money comes to me easily, and effortlessly". Here are some examples of positive self-talk.

- I am loving, lovable, and loved
- I look forward to each day
- I am worthy of love
- I am open to positive change
- Each day is an opportunity
- I make good choices
- I am beautiful inside and out
- I enjoy the magic in life
- I am responsible for my own life
- I forgive others and myself

- I am calm and relaxed
- I deserve good things
- I am worthy of respect and love
- I am special
- I treat myself and others with kindness
- I am interesting and interested
- I am attractive
- I attract wonderful people into my life

I reward myself regularly.
I allow myself to receive
nice things in my life.

REWARD YOURSELF 4

I t is important that you reward yourself on a regular basis in order
to achieve a more satisfying and happy life. These rewards need
not cost a lot of money, and in some instances, these rewards
cost no money at all! I suggest that you take the time out to reward
yourself two to three times per week. Rewarding yourself is also a
common distraction strategy to reduce or abstain from alcohol or
other drug use. Make the time to do at least two rewarding activities
each week.

- Treat yourself to a nice meal, or
  buy some special food
- Have a warm bath
- Have a special coffee or tea
- Go to an art gallery
- Take some time out alone
- Do absolutely nothing for
  an hour
- Take time to read a book or
  magazine
- Buy yourself something you have
  always wanted
- Enjoy a walk in nature
- Go for a swim
- Watch a good movie
- Take a walk on the beach
- Sit in a garden and relax
- Do yoga
- Sleep in on a Sunday and spend
  some time in bed

I make the most of my
five senses. I enjoy nature,
and being in the now.

SENSORY THERAPY 5

We human beings can really take our five senses for granted. That is sight, smell, hearing, touch, and taste. Make a conscious effort to tune into your senses from time to time. For example:

Sight

When was the last time you really appreciated nature around you? We can get so busy in our day-to-day lives that we can fail to notice the scenery that surrounds us. What about the sky, the clouds, the trees, birds, the beach, and rainforests? Or simply look at some flowers and leaves, and note the intricate nature of their appearance.

Smell

When was the last time you really smelt the roses, so to speak? How about walking in a wooded area and breathing in the earthy smells of nature? Breathe in the fresh smell of salt water when at the beach. Wear a special perfume/ aftershave, lotion, or oil. Enjoy the beautiful aroma of food, such as a roast dinner, bread, or cake.

Hearing

Who doesn't like the sound of rain on an iron roof when you are inside your home, cosy and warm? Better still, in bed at night. How about tuning into the sounds of nature such as birds, the wind, or perhaps distant ocean waves?

Touch

There's nothing like getting into some comfortable clothing and relaxing. Also, enjoy the simple things in life, such as a lovely shower or bath. Feel the warm soothing water against your skin, and wash yourself lovingly. How about the feel of fresh sheets on your bed? How long has it been since you have had a back, shoulder, neck, or foot massage?

Taste

What is your favourite food in the whole world? What is your favourite cold or hot drink? What meals make you feel healthy or comforted? Why not treat yourself to your favourite food occasionally, or a special food? How about fresh organic fruit, vegetables, or herbs? Perhaps try growing some of your own.

NOTES

I visualise what I want
in my life, and I create
the life I want to live.

VISUALISE WHAT YOU WANT IN LIFE   6

Thoughts are creative. What we believe, we can conceive! I want you to spend half an hour to one hour each day thinking about and picturing (i.e., visualising) exactly what you want in your life. Perhaps you might choose to focus on what you want to happen during the day, or within the next month, or next year. Or perhaps you want to be a little more specific (e.g., you might visualise the right romantic partner for yourself). It's up to you as to what you choose to think about. A great time to do visualisation is in the morning before you get out of bed (it might be an idea to set your alarm a little earlier than usual). Alternatively, you might want to set aside some time during the day for your visualisation, or perhaps before you go to bed. As an example, I set aside half an hour for visualisation today and this is what I thought about—a waterfront home. So for this visualisation, I imagined what this home would look like from the outside. That is, white, two story, ultra modern, lots of steel, tinted windows, a great big pool not far from my private jetty and a black and white powerboat. Last but not least, I visualised myself in the picture. There I was lying on a sun lounge in a nice swimming costume and sunglasses, sipping an icy cold fruit drink.

I write down my goals,
and I work towards them.
I have both short- and
long-term goals. I call
these my 'dreams'.

WRITE DOWN YOUR GOALS 7

G oals help to clarify what we want in our lives, and can make the steps to achieving what we want more systematic and achievable. Often, to achieve long-term goals, we need to take individual steps to get to the point of achievement, and these steps often entail short-term goals. Setting day-to-day goals is also important in that these goals help us to complete practical tasks that need doing. The completion of these goals can often give us a sense of achievement for each day. Goals give us something to work towards, and look forward to. Having goals and completing goals can make us push ourselves just that little bit further, instead of going along with life. Some people feel a little superstitious about goals. For example, "If I set a goal and I do not achieve it, then I will be disappointed". Don't let this form of negative thinking stop you from getting what you want in your life. You could think about weekly, monthly, 1-year, 2-year, 5-year, and 10-year goals. Perhaps you might just want to focus on general goals. See sample table.

Long-term Goals	Short-term Goals (Steps to achieving long-term goals)
1) Travelling overseas	1) Save $100 per week, which accumulates to $5200 by the end of the year. 2) Going through the house, room by room, and having a garage sale to get rid of unwanted items. 3) Selling some goods online. 4) Doing some tutoring to earn some extra money. 5) Doing some pamphlet deliveries to earn extra money.
2) Owning my own home	1) Putting away money each week for a deposit. 2) Looking into first homeowners' scheme. 3) Doing a budget, and working out exactly how much money is going out each week. 4) Designing a new budget. 5) Getting rid of things I don't need such as cable television.
3) Losing weight	1) Making sure I have a walk at least five times a week. 2) Looking into my diet to see where I can improve. 3) Cutting down or eliminating alcohol from my diet for a while. 4) Looking into gym membership, or exercise groups. 5) Cutting out take-away foods.

NOTES

A dream board helps
me manifest what I
want in my life.

CREATE A DREAM BOARD 8

P urchase a cork or magnetic board. Collect pictures of the sorts of things you love, and want in your life. Cut these pictures out and put these pictures on your 'dream board'. Make sure the dream board is in a prominent position in your home. For example, if you happen to spend a lot of time in your home office, you might want to put it above your desk. Alternatively, you might want to put it in your bedroom so as you can spend a few moments looking at it when you wake each day. On my dream board I have some wonderful pictures of what I want. There's the waterfront home with a jetty and a boat. There's a picture of a black BMW. There are also pictures of food I love to eat such as prawns, lobster, crab, mussels, and oysters. Lastly, there are pictures of places I would like to visit, such as as Italy, Sri Lanka, the Greek Islands, and all sorts of tropical destinations. Keep adding to your dream board, and if some of the pictures no longer appeal to you or you have achieved these objectives, then replace them with some new pictures.

I allow myself some
relaxation time every
day. It replenishes me.

SET ASIDE SOME TIME TO RELAX EACH DAY

9

S o often in life we are 'on the go,' doing daily activities such as taking the children to school, going to work, picking children up, cooking meals, washing and so on, and relaxation may fall by the wayside. Sometimes we mistake throwing ourselves on the lounge in front of the television at the end of the day as relaxing. However, the very nature of the typical programs on television, for example, shows about crimes, the news, current affair shows and so on, are usually quite sensationalised. These shows are far from relaxing! There are many ways to set aside a few moments a day to relax.

Hints to facilitate relaxation

- Practice at a regular time each day.
- Wear comfortable clothes.
- Take the telephone off the hook, and tell others around you that you will be setting aside some time to relax. Ask not to be disturbed.
- Sit in a chair or lie down (although lying down may increase the chance of falling asleep).
- Remove your shoes and socks.

The Slow Breathing Technique

Breathe in for 3 seconds, and then breathe out for 3 seconds. Say "relax" to yourself every time you breathe out. Let your breathing flow smoothly. Imagine the tension flowing out of your body each time you breathe out. Using this technique slows breathing down to 10 cycles per minute.

Progressive Muscle Relaxation

For each of the muscle groups in your body, tense the muscles for 7-10 seconds, and then relax for about 10 seconds. Only tense your muscles moderately (not to the point of inducing pain). You can start at any point in your body, but you might want to start from your head and work your way down to your toes. Starting with your head would entail tensing and relaxing facial muscles. For example, screw up your eyes, and then relax. Raise your eyebrow, and then relax. Screw up your mouth, and then relax and so on.

Imagery

Another relaxation technique involves imagining a relaxing scene. For example, you might imagine yourself under the shade of a palm tree on a sunny day, or perhaps in a rainforest listening to the sound of birds. You might just imagine yourself back at a favourite vacation spot, or at your local beach, or in the country. There are many imagery and progressive muscle relaxation Internet downloads available.

NOTES

I write down pros and cons
when making important
decisions, and the answer
becomes clear.

It's sometimes difficult to make choices (decisions) in life, as there are so many variables that can affect the outcome of what you decide (or what you don't decide!). It's often helpful to weigh up the pros and cons of a decision. There are a multitude of variables that can make decision-making confusing. One way of trying to illustrate the pros and cons of a decision is by completing a 'Decisional Balance Sheet'. Once completed, it's often easy to see what decision might work best. See this example:

Continue to stay in current job		Making a change to new job on offer	
Pros	**Cons**	**Pros**	**Cons**
• Familiarity	• Low pay	• Higher rate of pay	• Job security is not guaranteed
• Good relationships	• No pay rise on horizon	• Potential to advance to higher positions	• Slightly longer hours
• Job security	• Not challenging	• Good superannuation and salary sacrificing	

Once in a while, I set
aside a day just for me.
Life is short. It is not about
working all the time.

SET ASIDE A DAY FOR YOU 11

M en and women need time to rejuvenate and rest. Set aside a day when you can do wonderful things for you alone. It's a day of relaxation, not full of chores. It's a day for peace of mind, not worry. Each individual has different ideas of what a pampering day might entail, so it's up to you to design your pamper day. This design (i.e., a list of your plans for your pamper day) will need to be done a few days ahead of the pamper day. This preparation will ensure that you have all the supplies you need on hand.

This is a description of a possible pamper day—You make yourself some scrambled eggs, wholemeal toast, fresh orange juice, freshly made coffee, and enjoy it on a tray in bed. Then you might decide to have a bubble bath or perhaps a bath with an essential oil added, such as lavender or rosemary. Whilst you are in the bath, you might apply a facemask and conditioning hair treatment, either store bought or home made. Following your bath, make sure you have the newest version of your favourite magazine or book on hand, get into some comfortable clothing, and enjoy a herbal tea whilst reading your magazine or book. At lunchtime, prepare yourself a special healthy meal and a fresh juice or fruit smoothy. After lunch, settle on the lounge, perhaps with a day blanket if the weather is appropriate for snuggling, and put on a movie.

I can systematically solve problems by writing out steps for a solution.

PROBLEM-SOLVING EXERCISE 12

As with many mathematical equations, sometimes it's easier to write down a problem, and its possible solutions, rather than do it in your head! Sometimes when we try to solve problems, the possible solutions and options are difficult to weigh up. Sometimes we need to see the possible solutions in writing. The act of writing out a problem in terms of who is involved, what the problem is, when it occurs, and how it is normally dealt with is a useful start. We can then go on to look at possible solutions, and make solution focused decisions. This can lead us to see the problem more clearly, and then take steps towards solving the problem at hand. The following 'Problem-Solving Exercise' can be used to help solve a multitude of life's problems, both big and small. Get into the habit of using this format on a regular basis, and eventually it might be the case that problem-solving becomes easier and automatic for you. See example.

Who? (Who's involved in the problem)
→ My partner and myself.

What? (What is the problem)
→ Unfair distribution of labour in the home.

Where? (Where does this problem occur)
→ At home.

When? (When does this problem occur)
→ Each week.

How? (How do you normally deal with the problem)
→ I normally do everything myself but I get frustrated.

Pros and Cons of Problem?

• A **pro** would be continuing to do what I do so I don't 'rock the boat'.	• A **con** is that I feel jaded by the relationship, and mad at men in general, when I feel I am doing everything. • A **con** is that nothing is changing by not speaking up in order to negotiate a solution.

Solutions?

- Sit down with partner and talk about problem honestly.
- Decide on who will do what around the home on a weekly basis, and when this will occur.
- Think about trying to make this process more fun. For example, we might take turns at putting music on whilst we clean on a Saturday morning, or treat ourselves to breakfast at a café.

Solution Decision? (What solution works best)

❖ To implement the above steps.

Solution Steps? (Systematically list the steps needed to solve the problem)

1) Ask partner when he is free to have a talk.
2) Make a date to discuss issues.
3) Talk about the problem.
4) Ask partner for his input on possible solutions.
5) Type up a concrete plan.
6) Implement new plan.

NOTES

Diet and exercise is an important part of my daily routine. We need to remind ourselves that our bodies are like a fine machine. If we take care of the machine, it will last longer and work better.

DIET & EXERCISE

R esearch on the effects of physical exercise on mental health suggests that regular exercise can lead to the prevention, reduction, and management of depression. Exercise makes us feel good. Perhaps this is associated with the fact that exercise increases dopamine, a natural feel good brain neurochemical. There is increasing research on different reward circuits being activated by exercise. A vast body of research indicates exercise makes us feel good and helps us to look fitter and feel more energetic! You will likely feel great if you exercise for at least half an hour each day. This exercise might take the form of a walk, or a bike ride. Perhaps you would prefer yoga, tai chi, or a regular gymnasium routine. You might like to keep a diary of your exercise routine, and rate how you feel before and after each exercise session. This exercise will likely illustrate how wonderful exercise makes your feel. Alongside this diary, you might want to record the food you eat for breakfast, lunch, and dinner, along with any snacks between meals. This food and exercise diary is a way of becoming aware of your exercise and eating habits, and changing these habits to healthier ones if need be. The food diary also helps you monitor how each meal makes you feel, to give you an idea of what foods make you feel sluggish or negative, and what foods energise you or make you feel good. When reading the diary, imagine it belongs to someone else. Does this person's exercise or eating habits need improving? If so, what changes could this person make? Use a 0-100 rating system to rate the way you feel where 0= the worst possible feeling, and 100= the best possible feeling. See example.

Date	Food consumed	Feel good rating (0-100)	Exercise	Feel good rating (0-100)
10/03/13	**Breakfast (e.g.,)** • Toast and Vegemite • 1 boiled egg • Grapefruit juice • Peppermint tea	90	1 hour walk	95
	Lunch (e.g.,) • Vegetable burger on wholemeal roll with tabouli and a slice of cheese • 1 glass of fresh orange juice • 1 banana	100		
	Dinner (e.g.,) • Steamed chicken breast and salad • Steamed potato with sour cream • Date yoghurt and strawberries	95		
	Supper (e.g.,) • 4 wholemeal biscuits and cheese • 1 cup milk and honey	90		

NOTES

I look for the good in other human beings. Each and every human being has some good qualities.

LOOK FOR THE GOOD IN OTHERS AND YOURSELF 14

This exercise involves paying very close attention to those you come in contact with for a day. Over the course of a day, you might come in contact with various people such as friends and family, work colleagues, people who work at a shopping centre, and so on. I want you to note the positive qualities each person has. It might be the case that several of these people have helped you in some way over the course of the day. I want you to think about how these helpful people have made your day run relatively smoothly. I also want you to take note of all the good qualities you have. You might have caught a glimpse of yourself in the mirror this morning and appreciated what you saw, or maybe you washed your hair with a special shampoo and you have been appreciating the fresh scent of your hair. Make a mental note of all the positives you notice about yourself and others throughout the day. You might also want to acknowledge others by telling them about their good qualities you have observed, or by thanking them for helping you in some way. Some words that might describe the qualities you or others have might include:

- Honest
- Trustworthy
- Intelligent
- Caring
- Friendly
- Helpful
- Kind
- Loving

Dialogue writing is a
conversational exchange
with you, which can lead
to profound insights.

HAVE A CONVERSATION WITH YOURSELF 15

S ometimes it can really help to resolve personal issues or even practical problems by getting your thoughts down on paper. Even better, consider having a dialogue with yourself. Perhaps it is appropriate to refer to the 'wise you' in this conversation as the 'inner-self'. This process is very simple. First, you make a statement, or ask a question, and then the inner-self responds to the statement or answers the question/s. This technique is a very useful way of clearing out negative thoughts about particular life issues. Here is an example:

Tina: Gosh, why am I still single? I feel like I've been single forever! I wonder if this means I'm unlovable or unattractive.

Inner Self: Well Tina, you haven't exactly made any real efforts to meet single men for some years. Perhaps it's just the case that you have not been motivated in that aspect of life.

Tina: Yes, I guess so. It would be nice to have some company sometimes.

Inner Self: Yes, you have been spending a lot of time alone. Why don't you consider the idea of looking for a partner?

Tina: I guess I could . . . I wouldn't know what to do though! And starting a conversation can be so awkward! I've got nothing much to say anyway. Maybe I'm boring?

Inner Self: Now look Tina, you are far from boring. In fact, you are a very interesting person, and I'm sure a lot of people would love to find out more about you.

Tina: Yes, I guess so. I have had a lot of different life experiences, and some very interesting ones at that. I'm also easy to talk to, and good company.

Inner Self: Yes, I agree! Now what are you going to do in order to meet a partner?

Tina: Well, I guess I could tell a few friends and close work colleagues that I'm going to start dating. Perhaps they might have someone they know in mind, or perhaps they can give me some ideas on how to meet a suitable partner.

Inner Self: Great! What else?

Tina: Well, I guess I could give Internet dating a go. Apparently it can be quite successful, especially for those people who include photos. I could get a friend to take a recent photo of me.

Inner Self: Now that's a plan! It sounds like a great idea. Any other ideas?

Tina: Well, I never go out socially anymore. I guess it's unlikely that a potential partner will come knocking on my door out of the blue (although it has been known to happen!). I will make a commitment to accept all social invitations I receive. Even if I'm not enjoying myself, I can always stay for an hour and come home. You never know, I might become quite the socialite!

Inner Self: I'm with you all the way! This is going to be a wonderful adventure.

NOTES

Cooking can be therapeutic.
I put love into my cooking,
and my family and friends
appreciate my efforts.

COOKING THERAPY   16

S et aside some time, perhaps on a weekend, to really get stuck
into enjoying the cooking process. Perhaps you would like
to do a baking session (e.g., baking cookies, cakes, a roast
and vegetables). Perhaps you would like to try your hand at cooking
seafood. For example, you can cook fish, oysters, mussels, lobster, or
crab. Perhaps you would like a dessert session (i.e., making a lovely
Tiramisu, cheesecake, Pavlova, or Pana Cotta). Perhaps you would
like to plan a meal, based on a specific cuisine (e.g., Indian, Thai,
Japanese, Chinese, Mexican, African, and so on). Even better, cook
with other people, such as your children, a partner, friends etc. You
could plan a wood fire pizza night with everyone making his or her
own delicious creations. Perhaps invite special friends to bring their
favourite meal to share, or perhaps someone brings a course each
(e.g., entrée, main, a salad or vegetables, and lastly a dessert). Enjoy
the cooking process. Enjoy sharing food with family and friends.

One day I wrote down
my perfect workday on a
piece of paper. Later in
life I found the piece of
paper and I realised I was
living the life I wanted.

YOUR PERFECT WORK DAY 17

I want you to imagine and write about your perfect workday. In sum, how would you like your work-life to look ideally? Would it be fast paced or leisurely? Would you work from home, or would you work in an office, or other type of building? I want you to think about where you would be situated, what you would like to be doing, and importantly, run through your perfect workday. It is important to write about this workday. Here is an example of a perfect workday:

> I would make the children breakfast, a cup of green tea for me, and then shower and drive the children to school. I would come home and have a leisurely breakfast; perhaps something like smoked salmon, avocado, or paté on toast. I might read the paper or gaze out at the pristine pool whist eating my breakfast. I would then take a long walk on the beach. I live by the beach, so appreciating and enjoying a daily beach walk is important to me. I would come home and continue writing my next book. I would then have a leisurely lunch, and perhaps a few laps in the pool, and a bit of reading time for me. In the afternoon I would continue writing my book for a while, and then pick the children up from school. We would arrive home, have a fresh juice, and then take the dogs for a walk on the beach. We would then do some homework whilst I prepare a delicious dinner, and retire for the evening with a red wine and movie, or hop into bed after a nice bath and read a good book.

I love to pack a picnic.
I include some healthy
food, drinks, a rug, pillows,
and a good book.

PAMPER PICNIC

G et out that old picnic basket, add a rug, some sunscreen and a hat, some reading material such as books or magazines, perhaps some uplifting music, some yummy fresh food such as sandwiches, wraps, rolls, sushi, fruit, and cold drinks. Then go to the beach, a local park, a lake, a scenic reserve—whatever place takes your fancy. Perhaps take some pillows or fold-up deck chairs so you can really lounge around and make a day of it. Allow yourself to relax. It's good to get out of the house into the fresh air, where you can appreciate and enjoy the scenery. You can do this activity alone, with your family, or friends. Don't forget to pack some swimmers and a towel if you are by the water. This activity is not only refreshing and relaxing, but also free. You have got to eat anyway right? So why not eat out in the great outdoors. You might even find that the food tastes better when consumed outdoors. Pampering yourself does not have to cost a lot of money. A pamper picnic can be an economical, and pleasurable way to spend a relaxing day.

We all benefit from doing some positive activities in our lives. Do something different for a change. It's like 'a breath of fresh air'.

INCREASE POSITIVE ACTIVITIES   19

I ncreasing positive activities can have a multitude of terrific benefits. For example, increasing positive activities is good for decreasing depression, anxiety, and stress. Increasing positive activities is also commonly used as a distraction strategy if you have stopped smoking, or if you are trying to reduce or abstain from alcohol or other drug use. On the whole, if you make an effort to increase positive activities in your life you will just feel great! Here are some examples of some positive activities that you can incorporate into your weekly routine. Now, a word of warning, don't overdo it and exhaust yourself; rather the goal is to simply pick a few of these activities for the week and do them. Here are some questions to help generate a list of positive activities:

Activities I like to do alone?

• Watch a film, read, do some art and craft, or walk on the beach. I would like to visit natural environments and be mindful of the sights before me.

Activities I would like to do with a partner?

• Go for a coffee or for a meal, go to the movies, or a quiet night at home. I would also like to go to an occasional concert or show.

Activities I would like to do with a good friend/s?

- Go away for the weekend on occasion. I would like to invite friends over for breakfast, lunch, a dinner party, a bonfire, or a BBQ.

Activities I would like to do with groups?

- Join a yoga group, do an art class, and/ or join a cycling group. I would also like to see if there is a local walking group.

Community activities I would like to participate in?

- I would like to find out more about joining a conservation group. I would like to do some volunteer work at an animal shelter. I would also like to regularly pick up rubbish on the local beach.
- I have always wanted to crochet. I would like to knit more. I would also like to join a local book club. I would also like to try pottery.

NOTES

Pets are emotionally
rewarding. Most people
love animals. Spending
time with a pet can be very
therapeutic and positive.

SPEND A FEW HOURS WITH A PET 20

If you have a pet, spend some quality time enjoying their company. For example, if you have a dog, take it for a leisurely walk on the beach. Make sure you take lots of water for the both of you. How about going to a dog friendly café, or maybe just spend some time at home together on the lounge having cuddles. Perhaps you have a cat? Cuddle up on the lounge together for a nap, or perhaps grab a spot in the backyard and soak up a bit of gentle sunlight. You might even have a bird. Teach it to talk if the breed permits, or just spend some time whistling together. Alternatively, you might just want to be mindful (i.e., in the moment), and take in the beauty and characteristics of your beautiful bird. It might be the case that you have fish. Enjoy watching them swim in their tank. Just watch, be in the moment, and relax! Pets are therapeutic and good company. If you do not have a pet, think about babysitting a pet for a friend or family member for a few hours or days, or foster a pet.

Get in touch with nature by getting out in your own garden. Enjoy organic herbs, vegetables, and fruit from your own backyard.

GARDEN THERAPY 21

I t took me some time to truly appreciate the joy people get out of gardening, and at last I finally get it! It is the satisfaction of planting something, watering and fertilising it, watching it grow, and getting joy from this process. I love to grow herbs, fruit, and vegetables. In our garden we have herbs such as sage, coriander, parsley, chives, and mint. We have mulberries, blueberries, oranges, lemons, limes, mandarins, mangoes, bananas, and avocados. However, our pride and joy are three large corrugated iron vegetable beds filled with tomatoes, lettuces, silverbeet, cucumber, and Chinese vegies. We also have a couple of chickens that roam the garden by day. These little characters give us a regular supply of organic eggs. Our goal is to be as self-sufficient and organic as possible. Why not give gardening a go?

Water is such good
therapy. Enjoy cool water
on a hot day, or warm
water on a cold day.

WATER THERAPY

22

Make a point of spending the day, or part of the day, with water. There are quite a few options. For example, you could spend some time at a pool, a lake, have a relaxing bath, enjoy an invigorating shower, go to a natural spa or day spa, or soak your feet in a tub of warm water. Alternatively, walk in water barefoot for a few kilometres at the beach, or go for a swim at the beach. There are a number of options, depending on the weather, and the season. You could even take a walk in the rain. This could be with or without an umbrella! Have you ever been caught out in the rain without an umbrella? It's probably not the best experience at the time. That is, trying to get home whilst soaking wet, but what about when you get home? Your home feels warm, and perhaps you strip off the soaking wet clothes, and hop into a nice warm shower, and then dress in some comfortable clothing. How about a hot summer's day? There is nothing like a dip in a body of water, or drinking icy cold water. Enjoy water! After all, a large proportion of our bodies are made of water.

I try not to look at life's
challenges as negative.
I know that challenges
are a natural part of life.
These challenges help me
grow as a human being.

ACCEPT CHALLENGES

23

It seems that we often hope that life will go smoothly. If we were to illustrate this, perhaps we wish life were like a straight line. How realistic is this though? Everyone faces challenges, both big and small, and perhaps life is more like a wavy line, rather than a straight line. Our lives are full of challenges, and perhaps challenges help us grow. We can all grow spiritually, if we allow ourselves to. When we have challenges in our lives, often our problems can seem paramount. Sometimes we can make our problems bigger by catastrophising, by talking about the problem/s too much, and worrying too much. The good news is—most problems in life pass. In a week from now, a month from now, 6 months from now, a year from now—will you still have the same problem? Sometimes with minor problems, a problem this week is not a problem next week. Perhaps next week will presents us with new challenges. Problems can be 'water under the bridge', with the passing of time. Time can be a great healer and teacher. Take a new approach to accept challenges.

I accept other people just
as they are. Sometimes
I try to see things from
their perspective, and it
softens my heart a little.

ACCEPTANCE OF OTHERS 24

Sometimes it's difficult for us to understand other human beings. We can sometimes expect people to think like we do, or act like we do, or treat us the way that we treat them. Are these expectations realistic though? The thing is, people do not always treat us the way we treat them. Sometimes human beings can be irrational, 'bad', self-serving, downright rude, and so on. Perhaps we need to be more realistic, and accept that this is the case. The justice system, for example, is a human construct, designed to ensure fair outcomes. But does this really go to plan in reality? Sometimes outcomes can be fair, and sometimes unfair. Once we accept this, then perhaps we can get less stuck on some perceived or real injustices. Change your expectations of others treating you the way you treat them. Let that idea go. We all have negative experiences with others at times. We can't avoid all negative interactions, but we can choose to surround ourselves with trustworthy, loving humans in our lives, so that the negative interactions bother us less.

I know that I am not
perfect. No one is perfect.
Nothing is perfect. I accept
myself 'warts and all'.

ACCEPT IMPERFECTION

25

W hy is it that we can sometimes expect perfectionism from ourselves or even others? Who said that we have to do things perfectly? Who says anyone has to do things perfectly? No one is perfect. Nothing in life is perfect. Everyone and everything has flaws. However, should we be seeing these flaws as unique characteristics, or beauty marks? We should always aim to do things well, or perhaps try our best, but this does not mean that the outcome of our efforts needs to be perfect. Let go of perfectionism from now on. Whilst there are some good points associated with perfectionism, it can sometimes do more harm than good. Here are some pros and cons of perfectionism.

Pros of Perfectionism	Cons of Perfectionism
• Good work ethic	• Procrastination
• A job well done	• Self-criticism
• Achieves goals	• Anxiety
	• Depression
	• Frustration with self and others
	• Not attempting things in fear of failing
	• Not following through with tasks
	• Low self-esteem
	• Poor sense of wellbeing

I accept my life experiences.
I accept the fact that life has
not panned out in the way I
had planned. Although it has
not been perfect, I would
not change it for the world.

26

L ife can involve interesting and often challenging experiences (to put it mildly!). Each of us goes through a series of life experiences. No life experience is exactly the same. Sometimes we have conscious or unconscious expectations of ourselves, or expectations of our lives. Perhaps we had expectations about our first kiss, our first relationship, our first sexual experience, our first marriage, and so on. But the thing is, life rarely lives up to our expectations. How about the picket fence fantasy of meeting 'the one', marrying, buying a home, settling down, having children, and staying with that partner for life? About 50 percent of marriages end in divorce, so we have to ask ourselves whether our expectations are realistic. Life does not always go to plan. Life can be disappointing. The main thing we can get out of life is to grow and learn from our life experiences. Perhaps we can consider that every individual we come across in life teaches us something, big or small. Perhaps there are no 'mistakes' in life, only life experiences that shape us as spiritual beings.

I accept and appreciate my appearance. I don't get stuck on flaws. We are spiritual beings in human bodies. Our bodies are merely the vessels that carry us.

ACCEPT YOUR APPEARANCE 27

It's good to take care of our physical appearance, so long as we do not obsess about having the perfect physical appearance. We might not look the same as models in magazines, but we have to remind ourselves that the pictures of models have been airbrushed, and touched up. We also have to remind ourselves that models are freaks of nature, and that we mere human beings do not have to look like them. Take pride in your appearance, and take care of your physical body, but also remind yourself that you are much more than your physical body. You are a spiritual being within your body. You have much more essence and depth than physical appearance. We could think of our bodies as the vessels that carry our spirit.

Remind yourself that your physical body is only one part of you. Let others get to know and appreciate the whole 'you'. Importantly you need to accept yourself as you are. True self-love is when we accept ourselves 'warts and all'. Self-love is when we are kind to ourselves, and accept ourselves inside and out. Stop beating yourself up about perceived physical flaws, and learn to enjoy life without negative thoughts about physical appearance. You are beautiful inside and out. Start believing it.

Writing self-nurturing letters
to myself has felt incredibly
comforting and kind.

A LETTER FROM THE NURTURING YOU 28

W hy not write a special letter to yourself from your nurturing
self? We all need some nurturing and love sometimes.
There is absolutely nothing wrong with giving that love
to ourselves. For example:

Dear John,

It's been a while since I have actually checked in with
you to see how you are. How are you? How are you really
feeling right now? What can I do to help? I think you
might need to make sure you have some time out for you
sometimes. Just a little bit of time here and there in your
busy schedule. You might want to make sure that you get
out for a walk once a day, and it's also important that you
treat yourself to nice things in your life now and again.
Sometimes we can take care of others, but forget to take
care of ourselves as well. You are a special person, and I
want you to make nurturing yourself a part of your day,
a part of your week, a part of your month, a part of your
year. Nurturing and self-care is equally as important for
men and women.

Love from the nurturing you.

Everyone's life is interesting.
Everyone has a life story. Why
not write your life story today?

WRITE A BOOK ABOUT YOUR LIFE 29

E veryone's life is interesting. Every life is very different. Everyone
has a story. Why not write the story of your life from the very
beginning, right up until the present day. In effect you will be
writing the story so far, and then the next step might be to think
about how you will write (or create) the next chapters, or even the
final chapters of your life. This narrative approach reminds us that
we are the creators of our story in some ways. Well, our childhoods
may have been out of our control, but certainly as adults we are now
in control of the narrative of our lives. Here's an example of a story:

> My name is Melanie O'Shea. I was born in Surry Hills,
> Sydney, NSW, in 1971. I am an only child, but I always
> wanted a sibling. I grew up entertaining myself, and being
> very self-sufficient. I lived in Paddington, and other local
> children knew me as 'The Wanderer', as I would wander
> around the neighbourhood. We later moved to Annandale
> and I went to a Catholic School called St Brendan's. Later,
> my stepfather and my mother decided that we would live
> in Yowie Bay. It was quite some way from school at the
> time, St Scholastica's College at Glebe. Later we moved
> to the Blue Mountains. There was very little to do there.
> In my opinion it was just one arterial road, but I did meet
> friends who shaped my life in some way . . .

We have all had grievances
with others. It is amazingly
freeing to let go of
grievances rather than
carrying them for life.

WRITE AN UNSENT LETTER 30

Sometimes we have unresolved issues with people in our lives. It is not always possible to resolve issues in person for many reasons. The person may have passed on, or they might be alive, and just not responsive to resolving an issue and achieving some closure. Sometimes the best approach is to write an unsent letter. This is a letter to someone with whom you have a grievance, but you never actually send it. It is usually best left unsent, because this letter gives you the opportunity to get absolutely everything off your chest. You don't have to sensor your language, or be tactful in your approach, because the thing is, no one will ever get to read the letter aside from yourself (provided you keep it in a safe place!). When you have finished the letter it is up to you to do what you want with it. You may want to burn it. You may want to rip it up. Perhaps you would like to put it in a drawer, and re-read the letter in a month. If it still brings up emotions for you whilst reading it a month later, then put it in the drawer and re-read it in another month. Keep doing this until you no longer feel so emotional when reading the letter. This often means the issue has closure. You have moved on from the person you have a grievance with and you are free.

A FINAL WORD

I t has been an absolute pleasure sharing some techniques with you on how to achieve inner peace and live in the now. I would like to stress how important it is for all of us to make a commitment to our spiritual, psychological, and physical wellbeing. We need to nurture and care for ourselves, each and every day. Nurturing ourselves is not selfish, in fact if we are healthy emotionally and physically, then those around us benefit. We can attain a level of inner peace, and maintain this inner peace. Speaking of maintenance, it is not uncommon for individuals to read self-development books, but not put strategies into action. It is so important to make the effort to make positive changes in our lives. The old adage "actions speak louder than words" is so true. Make sure you take the action needed to improve your life. Life is short. This is not a dress rehearsal. Life does not go on indefinitely. Making the commitment to improve and maintain your wellbeing can be considered an essential to life, such as eating or sleeping. Make maintaining your wellbeing a part of your life from here on in. Change your thinking, take action, and reap the rewards. Live the totality of now, achieve some inner peace, and enjoy your life right now.

D r Melanie O'Shea was born in Australia, and spent 9.5 years at university completing four university degrees, culminating in a clinical psychology degree, and also a research PhD in biopsychology (behavioural pharmacology). After her many years of being a permanent student, she decided to relocate from New South Wales, to the Sunshine Coast in Queensland.

Dr O'Shea maintains a private practice where she treats a variety of psychological issues. She works with wonderful people, and finds it a pleasure to look at her diary each day, and see the names of the clients on her schedule. In her work as an author, she loves to share strategies for inner peace on a worldwide scale.

She lives with her family, and two Lhasa Apsos called Jedda and Monte. In terms of interests, she loves walking on the beach, and walking in general. She loves to cook for family and friends. In case you have not already guessed, she loves seafood in particular! She loves to read, watch movies, explore, relax, enjoy nature, and she has developed an appreciation of art.

Printed in the United States
By Bookmasters